MARKS &
SPENCER

thai

simple and delicious easy-to-make recipes

Lesley Mackley

Marks and Spencer p.l.c.
Baker Street, London, W1U 8EP

www.marksandspencer.com

ISBN: 1-84273-478-4

Printed in China

Produced by The Bridgewater Book Company Ltd

Photographer Simon Punter
Home Economist Ricky Turner

COVER
Photographer Ian Parsons
Home Economist Sara Hesketh

NOTES FOR THE READER

- This book uses both metric and imperial measurements. Follow the same units of measurement throughout; do not mix metric and imperial.
- All spoon measurements are level: teaspoons are assumed to be 5 ml, and tablespoons are assumed to be 15 ml.
- Unless otherwise stated, milk is assumed to be full-fat, eggs and individual vegetables such as potatoes are medium, and pepper is freshly ground black pepper.
- Recipes using raw or very lightly cooked eggs should be avoided by infants, the elderly, pregnant women, convalescents, and anyone suffering from an illness.
- Optional ingredients, variations or serving suggestions have not been included in the calculations. The times given are an approximate guide only. Preparation times differ according to the techniques used by different people and the cooking times may also vary.

contents

introduction

Thai cooking has become increasingly popular in the last few years. Most towns have at least one Thai restaurant, and the main ingredients, which not so long ago could be found only in specialist shops, have now become widely available.

Chillies are an essential ingredient in many dishes, and if you are not used to them, add them with caution. However, the use of coconut milk and fragrant herbs and spices has a cooling effect on the heat of the chillies. It should not be difficult to find the other ingredients used in these recipes, but if, for instance, fresh lemon-grass or lime leaves are unavailable, it will not affect the recipe if dried ones are used. Lemon-grass is also available in a purée. If you find fresh lime leaves and lemon-grass, it is worth stocking up, because they freeze very well. Fish sauce is the Thai equivalent to soy sauce and is used as a seasoning instead of salt. It gives a distinctive flavour to many Thai dishes, but if it is difficult to find, use soy sauce instead.

Many dishes in this book are suitable for vegetarians, and you can substitute soy sauce for fish sauce when the latter occurs in an otherwise vegetarian recipe. Thai cooking can be addictive, and once you are familiar with the ingredients and able to balance different flavours, you will enjoy adapting the recipes to your own taste.

guide to recipe key		
	easy	Recipes are graded as follows: 1 pea = easy; 2 peas = very easy; 3 peas = extremely easy.
	serves 4	Recipes generally serve four people. Simply halve the ingredients to serve two, taking care not to mix imperial and metric measurements.
	10 minutes	Preparation time. Where marinating or soaking noodles are involved, these times have been added on separately: eg, 15 minutes + 30 minutes to marinate.
	10 minutes	Cooking time.

hot chilli relish with crudités
page 20

prawn & pineapple curry
page 28

peanut crusted chicken with dipping sauce
page 56

thai bananas
page 90

soups, starters & snacks

In Thailand, soups usually stay on the table throughout the meal. They can serve as a sauce for rice or dishes that have no sauce of their own. Some soups, such as Hot & Sour Fish Soup, are very light and can be served as a first course, whereas others are more substantial and may be served as a light lunch or supper dish. Finger food, particularly when sold on the street, is very popular in Thailand. Snacks such as Spring Rolls, Chicken Satay or Hot Chilli Relish with Crudités (Nam Prik) can be served as a starter or as party food with drinks.

chicken & coconut milk soup

extremely easy	
serves 4	
10 minutes	
15 minutes	

ingredients

400 ml/14 fl oz canned coconut milk
500 ml/18 fl oz chicken stock
6 thin slices fresh galangal
2 stalks fresh lemon-grass, bruised
4 fresh kaffir lime leaves
225 g/8 oz chicken breast fillets,
   cut into strips

2 red chillies, deseeded and
   sliced finely
4 spring onions, sliced finely
4 tbsp fish sauce
2 tbsp lime juice
2 tbsp chopped fresh coriander

Place the coconut milk, chicken stock, galangal, lemon-grass and lime leaves in a large pan and bring to the boil.

Add the chicken, reduce the heat and simmer, uncovered, for 10 minutes, or until the chicken is cooked.

Add the chillies and spring onions and simmer for 3 more minutes.

Stir in the fish sauce, lime juice and coriander and serve immediately, in warmed bowls.

hot & sour
prawn soup

		ingredients	
	very easy	500 g/1 lb 2 oz large raw prawns, in shells	STOCK
		55 g/2 oz oyster mushrooms, sliced thinly	450 g/1 lb white fish bones
	serves 4–6		2 litres/3½ pints water
		2 tsp light soy sauce	2 stalks of fresh lemon-grass, chopped finely
		1 tsp white sugar	2–4 small dried red chillies
	30 minutes	4 spring onions, sliced finely	4 fresh or dried kaffir lime leaves
		2 tsp fish sauce	2.5 cm/1 inch fresh root ginger, peeled
	30 minutes	2 tbsp chopped fresh coriander	2 slices of fresh or dried galangal

To make the stock, peel the prawns and place the shells in a large saucepan with the fish bones, water, lemon-grass, chillies, lime leaves, ginger and galangal. Bring to the boil, reduce the heat and simmer, covered for 20 minutes.

Strain the stock into another large pan. Add the prawns, mushrooms, soy sauce, sugar and spring onions. Bring back to the boil, then reduce the heat and simmer for 3 minutes, or until the prawns are cooked. Add the fish sauce and coriander, cook for 1 more minute, then serve immediately.

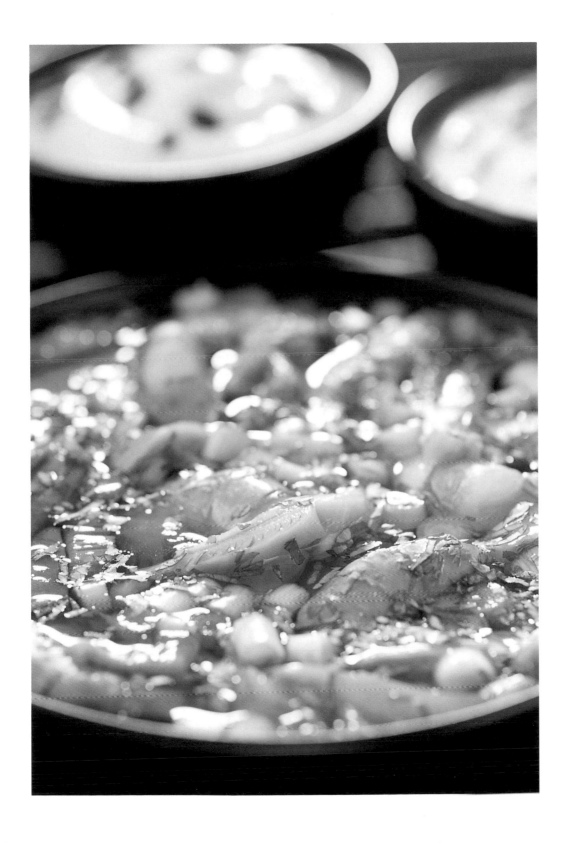

aromatic chicken
& vegetable soup

		ingredients	
	very easy	handful of fresh coriander	225 g/8 oz chicken breast fillet, diced
		1 litre/1¾ pints chicken stock	100 g/3½ oz mangetouts,
	serves 4	1 stalk fresh lemon-grass, bruised	cut into thin diagonal strips
		1 small fresh red chilli	1 carrot, shaved into ribbons
		grated zest and juice of ½ lime	100 g/3½ oz baby sweetcorn,
	15 minutes	salt and pepper	sliced thinly
			4 spring onions, sliced thinly
	30 minutes		

Strip the coriander leaves from the stalks. Reserve the leaves and place the stalks in a large pan with the stock, lemon-grass, chilli and lime zest. Bring to the boil, then reduce the heat and simmer, covered, for 15 minutes.

Strain the stock into another pan. Add the lime juice, and salt and pepper to taste.

Add the chicken to the stock. Bring to the boil, then reduce the heat and simmer for 5 minutes. Add the mangetouts, carrot and sweetcorn and simmer for about 2 minutes, or until the vegetables are tender and the chicken is cooked.

Roughly chop the coriander leaves and stir into the soup with the spring onions. Serve immediately.

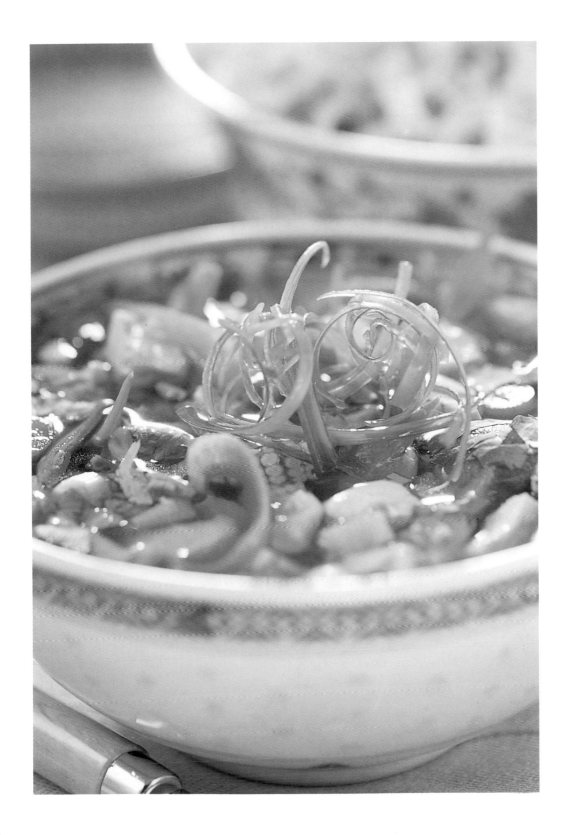

spring rolls

		ingredients	
easy	1 tbsp vegetable oil	2.5 cm/1 inch piece root ginger, grated finely
	250 g/9 oz lean minced pork	
	1 garlic clove, crushed	2 tbsp chopped fresh coriander
makes 30	1 red chilli, deseeded and chopped finely	2 tsp fish sauce
		30 spring roll wrappers
	115 g/4 oz cooked prawns, shelled and chopped	oil, for deep frying
20 minutes	2 spring onions, chopped finely	sweet chilli sauce, to serve
15 minutes (food cooked in batches)		

Heat the oil in a frying pan. Add the pork, garlic and chillies and cook, stirring until the pork is browned.

Add the prawns, spring onions, ginger, coriander and fish sauce. Cook, stirring, until heated through. Remove from the heat and set aside to cool.

Prepare the spring roll wrappers as directed on the packet.

Place a spoonful of the pork mixture down the middle of each spring roll sheet, leaving a space at the top and bottom and down the side. Brush the edges with water. Fold the top and bottom over and then fold in the sides to form a sealed roll.

Just before serving, heat the oil for frying in a large pan or wok until nearly smoking. Fry the rolls, in batches, for 2–3 minutes, or until golden brown. Drain on kitchen paper and keep warm while frying the remainder. Serve with sweet chilli dipping sauce.

chicken satay

		ingredients	
very easy	900 g/2 lb chicken breast meat, cut into 5 mm/¼ inch thick, 2.5 cm/1 inch wide strips	1 tsp ground cumin
serves 8 as a starter		1 tsp ground coriander
	MARINADE	1 tbsp lime juice
	2 tbsp vegetable oil	1 tsp soft light brown sugar
10 minutes + 1 hour to marinate	2 tbsp soy sauce	PEANUT SAUCE
	2 tsp tamarind paste	2 tbsp smooth peanut butter
	1 lemon-grass stalk (tender inner part only), chopped roughly	200 ml/7 fl oz coconut cream
10 minutes		2 tsp red Thai curry paste
	2 garlic cloves, crushed	1 tbsp fish sauce
		1 tbsp soft light brown sugar

Thread the chicken onto bamboo skewers.

To make the marinade, place the oil, soy sauce, tamarind paste, lemon-grass, garlic, cumin, coriander, lime juice and sugar in a food processor and blend to make a paste. Transfer to a bowl.

Add the chicken to the marinade and toss to coat. Cover with clingfilm and refrigerate for at least 1 hour to marinate.

To make the peanut sauce, put the peanut butter, coconut cream, red Thai curry paste, fish sauce and sugar in a pan. Heat gently, stirring, to form a smooth sauce.

Grill the chicken on a barbecue or under a grill for 3–5 minutes on each side, or until the chicken is cooked through. Reheat the sauce, adding a little hot water if necessary, and serve with the chicken satays.

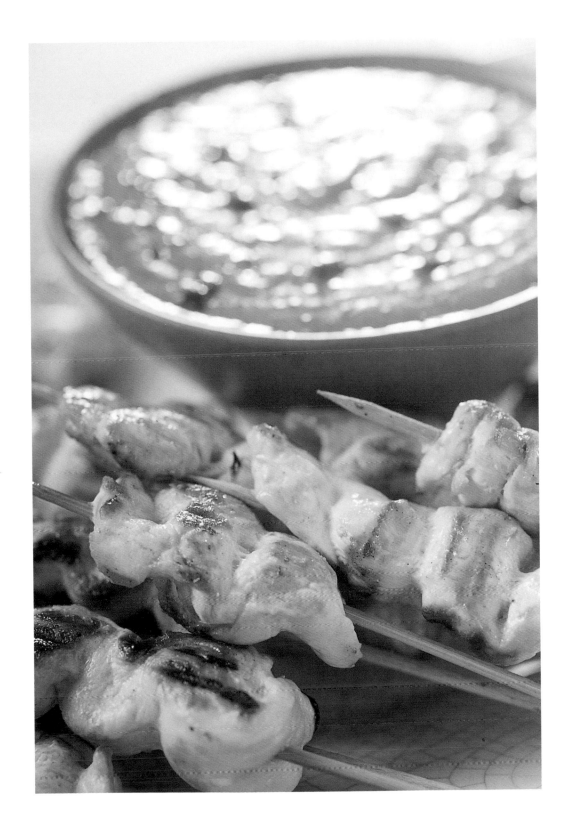

thai pork appetiser

		ingredients	
very easy		4 garlic cloves, chopped finely	2 tbsp fish sauce
		2 fresh red chillies, deseeded and chopped finely	1 tsp soft light brown sugar
serves 6		1 tbsp chopped coriander root	2 tbsp roughly chopped fresh coriander
		1 tbsp grated fresh ginger	
20 minutes		3 tbsp vegetable oil	GARNISH
		1 tbsp hot water	fresh coriander leaves
		500 g/1 lb 2 oz lean minced pork	thin strips of red chilli
20 minutes		2 fresh kaffir lime leaves, shredded finely	crisp lettuce cups, to serve

Place the garlic, chillies, coriander root, ginger, oil and water in a blender, then blend until smooth. Transfer to a wok or frying pan.

Heat and stir the paste for 4 minutes over a medium heat, then increase the heat and add the minced pork. Stir-fry for 3 minutes until coloured.

Add the lime leaves, fish sauce, sugar and chopped coriander. Continue to cook, stirring, until the pork is dry.

Serve the pork in lettuce cups, garnished with coriander leaves and strips of chilli.

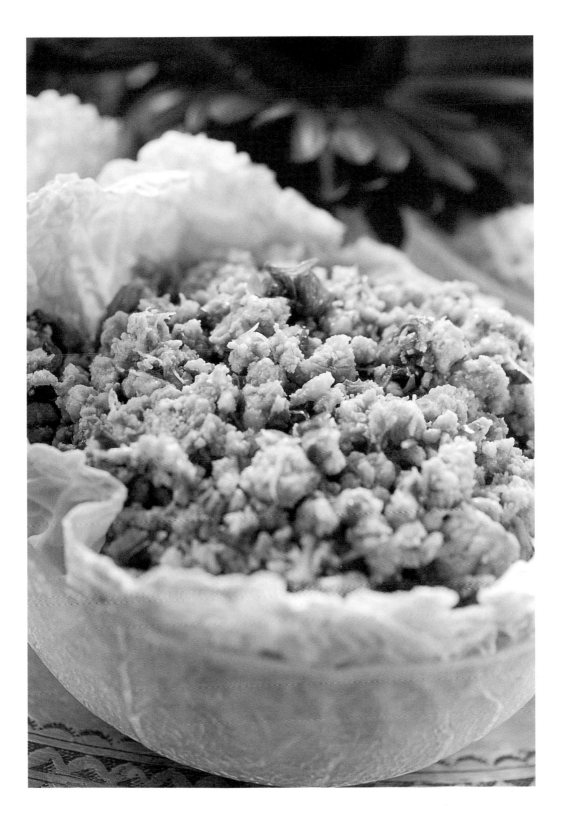

hot chilli relish
with crudités

		ingredients	
extremely easy		RELISH	SERVING SUGGESTIONS
		8–10 large red chillies, deseeded and chopped finely	carrot sticks
serves 4		6 garlic cloves, chopped finely	radishes
		125 ml/4 fl oz water	cucumber batons
		½ tsp salt	baby sweetcorn
10 minutes		2 tsp sugar	
		juice of 1 lime	
		1 tbsp fish sauce	
15 minutes		1 tbsp vegetable oil	

Put all the relish ingredients in a pan and bring to the boil.
Cover and simmer for 10 minutes.

Transfer the relish to a bowl and serve with vegetables.

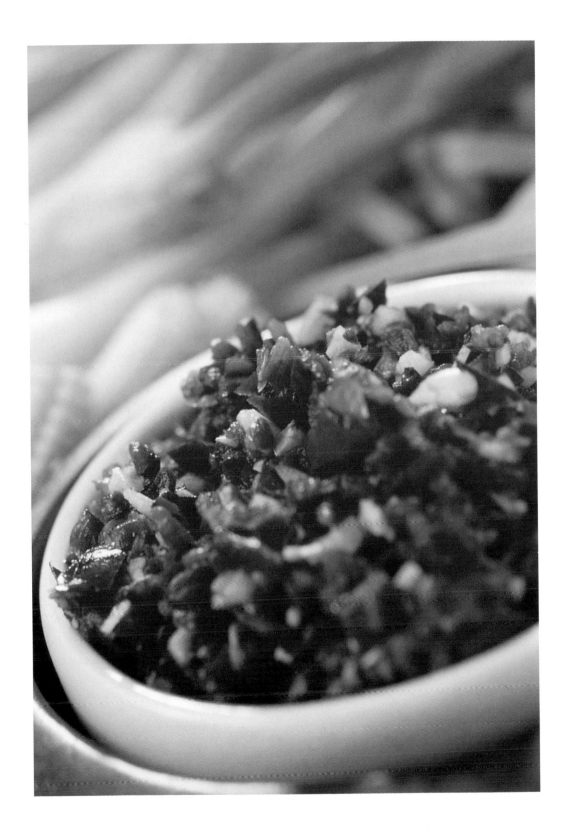

thai omelette

		ingredients	
very easy	6 eggs	2 tomatoes, peeled, deseeded and
	salt and pepper	cut into 1 cm/½ inch dice
serves 2	1 tbsp butter	2 tsp fish sauce
	1 tbsp oil	1 tsp sugar
		2 tsp lime juice
	FILLING	1 tbsp tomato ketchup
15 minutes	1 tbsp oil	4 spring onions, chopped finely
	1 small onion, chopped finely	
	1 garlic clove, crushed	
30–35 minutes	115 g/4 oz minced pork	salad, to serve
	100 g/3½ oz green peas	

To make the filling, first heat the oil in a frying pan. Add the onion and garlic and fry gently for 10 minutes, or until soft. Add the pork and fry, stirring, for 5 minutes, or until coloured.

Add the peas, tomatoes, fish sauce, sugar, lime juice, tomato ketchup and spring onions. Cook, stirring, for 10 minutes, adding a little water if the mixture is too dry.

In a bowl, whisk 3 of the eggs and season with salt and pepper.

Heat half the butter and oil in an omelette pan. Add the eggs and cook for 2–3 minutes, pulling in the edges with a fork and allowing any egg to run to the base of the pan.

When almost set, place half the filling mixture on one half of the omelette. Fold over and transfer to a plate. Keep warm while making the second omelette. Serve with salad.

fish
& seafood

Thailand has a long coastline and a large number of the people live near the sea. They have always made use of the abundance of fish and shellfish, and Thai cuisine includes many delicious recipes for fish, prawns, crabs and mussels. Traditional Thai dishes such as Fish Cakes and Prawn & Pineapple Curry are quick and easy to make using ready-made Thai fish sauce, while Tiger Prawn Skewers and Spiced Steamed Fish will liven up any dinner table.

thai fish cakes

		ingredients	
	very easy	500 g/1 lb 2 oz skinless, boneless	4 tbsp oil, for frying
		cod fillet, cut into chunks	lime wedges, to garnish
		1 tbsp red curry paste	
	serves 4	1 egg, beaten	SERVING SUGGESTIONS
		1 tsp light muscovado sugar	salad
	15 minutes	1 tsp salt	green beans
	+ 30 minutes	1 tbsp cornflour	broccoli
	to chill	75 g/2¾ oz green beans,	mangetouts
		chopped finely	
	30 minutes	1 tbsp chopped fresh coriander	

Put the cod into in a food processor and chop roughly. Add the curry paste, egg, sugar, salt and cornflour. Blend well.

Stir in the green beans and coriander.

Transfer to a bowl, cover with clingfilm and chill in the refrigerator for 30 minutes. Roll the mixture into 12 balls, then flatten each ball into a 5 cm/2 inch cake.

Heat the oil in a frying pan over a medium heat and cook the cakes in batches for about 3 minutes on each side, or until golden brown and cooked through. Keep the cooked fish cakes warm in a low oven while frying the remainder.

Garnish with the lime wedges and serve with salad or stir-fried green vegetables such as beans, mangetouts or broccoli.

prawn & pineapple curry

		ingredients	
extremely easy		450 ml/16 fl oz coconut cream ½ fresh pineapple, peeled and chopped 2 tbsp Thai red curry paste 2 tbsp fish sauce 2 tsp sugar	350 g/12 oz raw tiger prawns, shelled and deveined 2 tbsp chopped fresh coriander 4 spring onions, shredded, to garnish steamed jasmine rice, to serve
serves 4			
10 minutes			
10–15 minutes			

Place the coconut cream, pineapple, curry paste, fish sauce and sugar in a pan. Heat gently over a medium heat until almost boiling. Add the prawns and coriander and simmer gently for 3 minutes, or until the prawns are cooked.

Sprinkle with the shredded spring onions and serve with steamed jasmine rice.

thai fish curry

		ingredients	
easy		4 shallots, chopped roughly	½ tsp salt
		5 cm/2 inch fresh root ginger, peeled	400 ml/14 fl oz coconut cream
serves 4		and sliced finely	4 fish steaks, eg cod, turbot, halibut
		5 cm/2 inch fresh lemon-grass,	
		outer leaves discarded	GARNISH
		5 cm/2 inch fresh galangal, peeled	1 red chilli, cut into thin strips
20 minutes		and chopped finely	2 tbsp toasted flaked almonds
		3 red chillies, deseeded and	
		chopped roughly	TO SERVE
20 minutes		1 tbsp ground almonds	cooked white rice
		½ tsp turmeric	salad

Place the shallots, ginger, lemon-grass, galangal, chillies, ground
almonds, turmeric and salt in a blender. Add 6 tablespoons of the
coconut cream. Blend to a smooth paste.

Pour the paste into a large frying pan. Bring to the boil and cook,
stirring, for 4 minutes. Add the remaining coconut milk and bring
back to the boil.

Place the fish steaks in the pan and simmer for 10 minutes,
turning once, until the fish is cooked and flakes when tested
with a fork. If the sauce is too thin, transfer the fish to a heated
serving dish and boil the sauce to reduce to the desired
consistency. Garnish with red chilli and toasted almonds and
serve with rice and a salad of your choice.

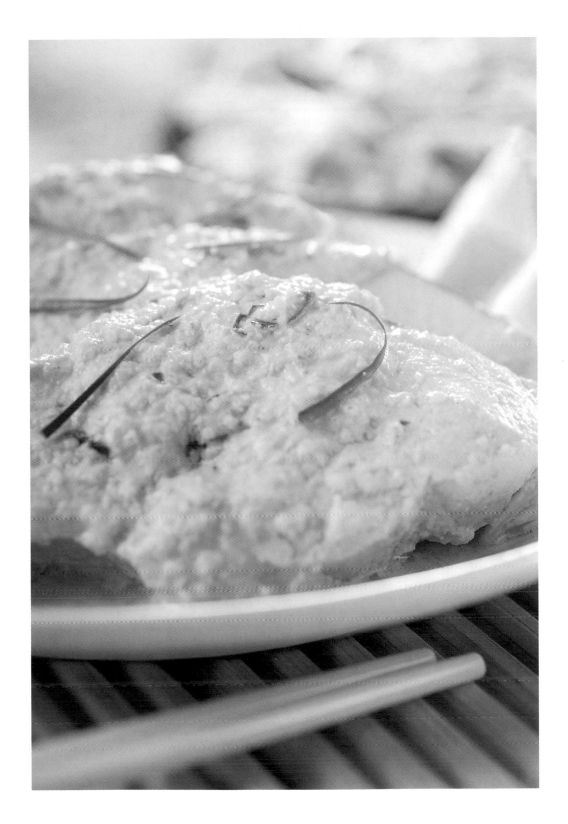

tiger prawn
skewers

easy	
serves 4 as an appetiser or 2 as a main dish	
15 minutes + 1 hour to marinate	
5 minutes	

ingredients

MARINADE
3 garlic cloves, crushed
2 shallots, chopped finely
2.5 cm/1 inch fresh root ginger,
   peeled and grated finely
1 lemon-grass stalk, chopped finely
1 fresh red chilli, chopped finely
pinch of salt
1 tbsp lime juice
1 tbsp soy sauce
2 tbsp rice wine or dry sherry

12 raw tiger prawns, in shells

GARNISH
coriander sprigs
lime wedges

3 oranges, to serve

To make the marinade, place the garlic, shallots, ginger, lemon-grass, chilli, salt, lime juice, soy sauce and rice wine or sherry in a blender and blend until smooth. Transfer to a shallow bowl.

Using a small knife, or scissors, split the prawn shells down the back, but leave attached. Devein if necessary. Add to the marinade. Cover with clingfilm and place in the refrigerator to marinate for 30 minutes to 1 hour.

Thread each prawn onto a bamboo skewer, inserting the skewer at the tail and coming out at the head end until the pointed end extends at least 7 cm/3 inches beyond the prawn.

Grill for 2 minutes on each side, or until the prawns are pink and cooked through. Garnish with the coriander sprigs and lime wedges. Stick the skewers in the orange, to serve.

spiced steamed fish

		ingredients	
very easy		2.5 cm/1 inch piece ginger, grated finely	2 kaffir lime leaves, sliced thinly
serves 4–6		1 lemon-grass stalk (base only), sliced thinly	2 sprigs fresh basil leaves
10 minutes		6 fresh red chillies, deseeded and chopped roughly	TO SERVE
		1 small red onion, chopped finely	cooked rice
		1 tbsp fish sauce	cucumber batons
20–25 minutes		900 g/2 lb whole fish (eg sea bass, red snapper, trout, tilapia), cleaned	

Place the ginger, lemon-grass, chillies, onion and fish sauce in a blender. Chop coarsely to a rough paste, adding a little water, if necessary.

Cut 3–4 deep slits crosswise on each side of the fish. Spread over the spice paste, rubbing it well into the slits.

Place the fish in a dish deep enough to hold the liquid that collects during steaming. Sprinkle over the lime leaves and basil.

Set up a steamer or put a rack into a wok or deep pan. Bring about 5 cm/2 inches of water to the boil in the steamer or wok. Put the dish of fish into the steamer or onto the rack. Reduce the heat to a simmer. Cover tightly and steam the fish for 15–20 minutes, or until the fish is cooked through. Serve with rice and cucumber batons.

fragrant mussels

easy	
serves 2–3 as a main course, 4–6 as a starter	
10 minutes	
15–20 minutes	

ingredients

1 kg/2 lb 4 oz mussels, cleaned
2 tbsp water
1 lemon-grass stalk, bruised
2 garlic cloves, crushed
3 fresh or dried kaffir lime leaves, chopped roughly

200 ml/7 fl oz coconut cream
2 tbsp chopped fresh coriander
salt and pepper

warm, crusty bread, to serve

Clean the mussels by scrubbing the shells and pulling out any beards that are attached. Rinse well, discarding any that are broken or remain open when tapped.

Put the water, lemon-grass, garlic and lime leaves in a large pan. Heat until boiling. Add the mussels, cover and cook for 5–6 minutes, or until they have opened. Discard any which stay closed. Transfer the mussels to a heated serving dish, cover and keep warm in a low oven.

Boil the cooking liquid hard until reduced by half, then stir in the coconut cream. Boil to reduce and thicken slightly. Stir in the coriander and season to taste.

Pour over the mussels and serve with warm, crusty bread.

meat
& poultry

Chicken and duck are widely used in Thai cooking. Many families keep their own chickens and ducks and, because they are free range, they tend to be smaller and tougher than the ones we buy. Most recipes, such as the traditional Green Chicken Curry, are quickly prepared in a wok. Pork is the most popular meat, but beef is also used in classical recipes such as Masaman Beef Curry. Lamb is becoming more popular and, in most of the recipes, the meat used can be varied to suit your taste. Also in this section are main course salads made with beef or duck.

grilled beef salad

		ingredients	
very easy	DRESSING	50 g/1¾ oz dried oyster mushrooms
	2 tbsp sesame oil	600 g/1 lb 5 oz rump steak
serves 4	2 tbsp fish sauce	1 tbsp vegetable oil
	2 tbsp sweet sherry	salt and pepper
	2 tbsp oyster sauce	1 red pepper, deseeded and
10 minutes + 20 minutes to soak mushrooms	1 tbsp lime juice	sliced thinly
	1 fresh red chilli, deseeded and	40 g/1½ oz roasted cashew nuts
	chopped finely	
5–10 minutes		red and green lettuce leaves, to serve
		mint leaves, to garnish

Place the mushrooms in a bowl, cover with boiling water and leave to stand for 20 minutes. Drain and cut into thin slices.

To make the dressing, place the sesame oil, fish sauce, sherry, oyster sauce, lime juice and chilli in a bowl and whisk to combine.

Grill the beef, either on a ridged iron grillpan or under the grill, turning once, for 5 minutes, or until browned on both sides and rare in the middle, or cook longer if desired.

Slice the steak into thin strips and place in a bowl with the mushrooms, pepper and nuts. Add the dressing and toss together.

Arrange the lettuce on a large serving platter and place the beef mixture on top. Garnish with mint leaves. Serve at room temperature.

thai beef curry

easy	
serves 4	
15 minutes	
1½–2 hours	

ingredients

3 tbsp vegetable oil
800 g/1 lb 12 oz braising steak, cubed
2 onions, sliced thinly
2 tbsp Thai red curry paste
1 tbsp tamarind paste or lime juice
2 tbsp fish sauce
850 ml/1½ pints coconut milk
2 tsp sugar

6 cardamom pods, crushed
1 small pineapple, peeled
   and chopped

TO SERVE
cooked rice
prawn crackers

Heat the oil in a flameproof casserole. Brown the beef in batches and set aside.

Add the onions to the oil and cook for 5 minutes, then set aside with the beef. Add the curry paste and cook gently for 1 minute, stirring constantly.

Stir in the tamarind paste, the fish sauce, coconut milk and sugar. Bring to the boil, then reduce the heat and return the beef and onions to the casserole with the cardamom.

Simmer gently, uncovered, for 1–1½ hours, or until the meat is tender. Stir from time to time and if it is becoming dry, cover with a lid.

Add the pineapple and cook for 5 more minutes. The curry should be quite dry, but add a little water if necessary.

Serve with rice and prawn crackers.

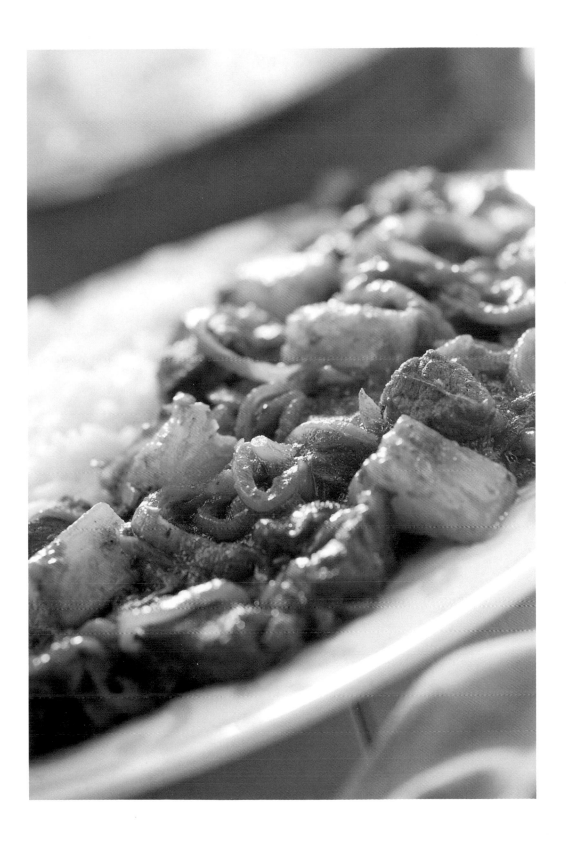

pork steaks
with lemon-grass

		ingredients	
extremely easy		MARINADE	4 spring onions, chopped finely
		2 garlic cloves, crushed	2 tbsp coconut milk
serves 4		½ tsp freshly ground black pepper	
		1 tbsp sugar	4 pork steaks
		2 tbsp fish sauce	
5 minutes + 1 hour to marinate		2 tbsp soy sauce	lime wedges, to garnish
		1 tbsp sesame oil	
		1 tbsp lime juice	TO SERVE
10 minutes		2 lemon-grass stalks, outer leaves removed, chopped finely	salad stir-fried vegetables

To make the marinade, place the garlic, pepper, sugar, fish sauce, soy sauce, sesame oil, lime juice, lemon-grass, spring onions and coconut milk in a large shallow dish and mix well to combine.

Turn the pork steaks in the marinade, cover the dish with clingfilm and place in the refrigerator for 1 hour.

Grill the pork steaks under a preheated grill or over charcoal, for 5 minutes on each side, or until cooked through. Garnish with lime wedges and serve with salad or stir-fried vegetables.

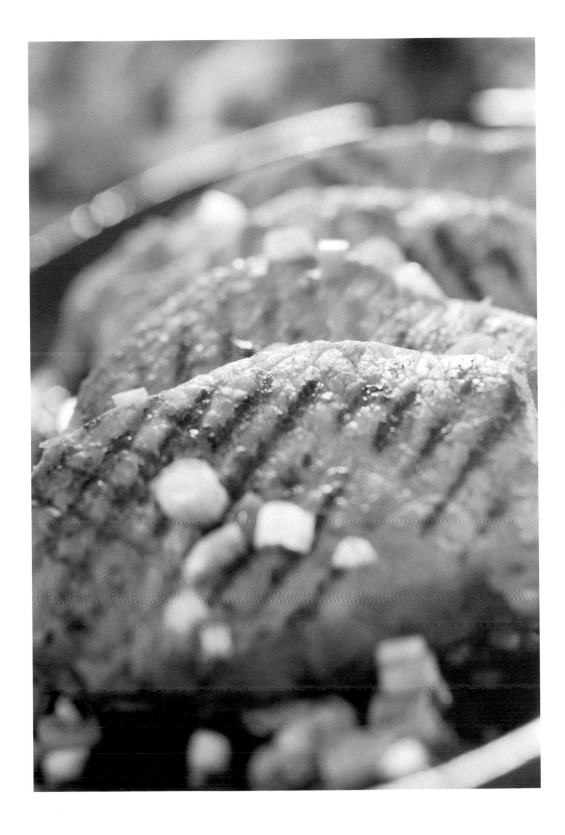

tamarind pork

very easy	
serves 4	
15 minutes	
8–10 minutes	

ingredients

SPICE PASTE
4 shallots, chopped finely
2 garlic cloves, chopped finely
2.5 cm/1 inch fresh ginger root,
  peeled and chopped finely
1 tsp ground coriander
2 fresh red chillies, deseeded and
  chopped finely
½ tsp ground turmeric
6 blanched almonds, chopped finely

2 tbsp tamarind paste
2 tbsp hot water

2 tbsp vegetable oil
600 g/1 lb 5 oz lean pork, cut into
  thin strips
225 g/8 oz canned bamboo shoots,
  drained

cooked noodles, to serve

To make the spice paste, place the shallots, garlic, ginger, ground coriander, chillies, turmeric, almonds, tamarind paste and water in a food processor and blend until smooth.

In a wok or frying pan, heat the oil over a high heat. Add the pork and cook for 3 minutes, or until the meat is coloured. Then add the spice paste and continue to cook for 2 or 3 more minutes.

Add the bamboo shoots and cook for 2 more minutes, or until the pork is cooked through. Serve with hot noodles.

stir-fried lamb
with mint

		ingredients	
easy			
serves 4	2 tbsp vegetable oil	225 g/8 oz canned baby sweetcorn,	
	2 garlic cloves, sliced finely	drained	
	2 fresh red chillies, deseeded and	4 spring onions, chopped finely	
15 minutes	cut into thin strips	25 g/1 oz fresh mint leaves,	
	1 onion, sliced thinly	shredded roughly	
	1½ tbsp madras curry paste	1 tbsp fish sauce	
30 minutes (food cooked in batches)	500 g/1 lb 2 oz lamb fillet, cut into thin strips	cooked rice, to serve	

Heat half the oil in a wok or large frying pan. Add the garlic and chilli and cook until soft. Remove and set aside. Add the onion and cook for 5 minutes, or until soft. Remove and set aside.

Heat the remaining oil in the wok, add the curry paste and cook for 1 minute. Add the lamb, in batches if necessary, and cook for 5–8 minutes, or until cooked through and tender.

Return the onion to the wok with the baby sweetcorn, spring onions, mint and fish sauce. Cook until heated through. Scatter the garlic and chilli over and serve with rice.

stir-fried chicken
with thai basil

		ingredients	
very easy			

<table>
<tr><td>very easy</td><td colspan="2">

2 tbsp vegetable oil
4 garlic cloves, crushed
4 spring onions, chopped finely
4 green chillies, deseeded and
  chopped finely
1 green pepper, deseeded and
  sliced thinly
600 g/1 lb 5 oz skinless, boneless
  chicken breast fillets, cut into
  thin strips
</td><td>

25 g/1 oz fresh Thai basil leaves,
  chopped roughly
2 tbsp fish sauce

basil leaves, to garnish

cooked rice, to serve
</td></tr>
</table>

serves 4

15 minutes

15 minutes

Heat the oil in a wok. Add the garlic and spring onions and cook for 1–2 minutes, or until soft.

Add the chilli and green pepper and cook for 2 minutes.

Add the chicken and cook until browned. Stir in the basil and fish sauce, and cook for a few more minutes, or until the chicken is cooked through. Garnish with basil leaves and serve with rice.

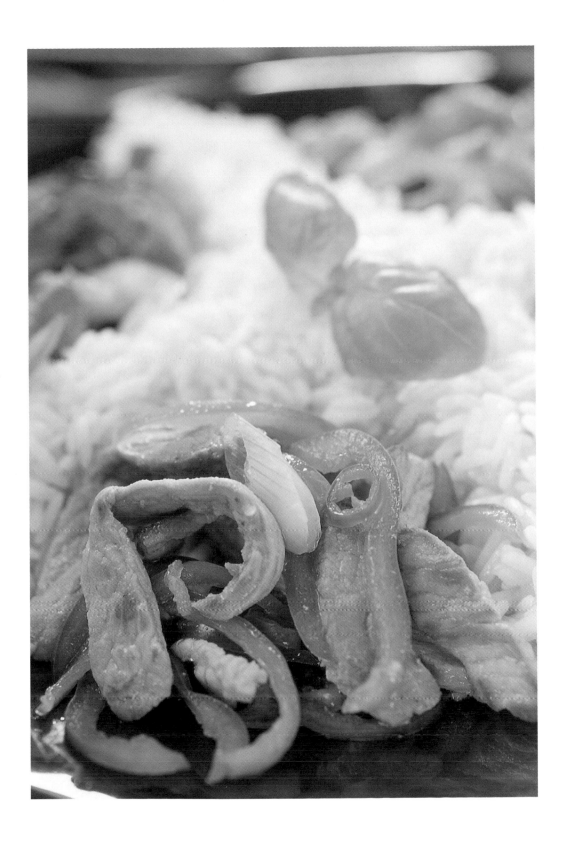

quick green
chicken curry

		ingredients
	extremely easy	1 tbsp vegetable oil 6 spring onions, sliced 600 g/1 lb 5oz skinless, boneless chicken breast, cut into cubes 200 ml/7 fl oz coconut cream 3 tbsp green Thai curry paste 3 tbsp chopped fresh coriander
	serves 4	
	5 minutes	
	10 minutes	cooked noodles or rice, to serve

Heat the oil in a large frying pan. Add the spring onions and the chicken and cook, stirring, for 3–4 minutes, or until the chicken is browned.

Stir in the coconut cream and curry paste and cook for 5 more minutes, or until the chicken is cooked through. Add a little water or stock if the sauce becomes too thick.

Stir in the chopped coriander and serve with rice or noodles.

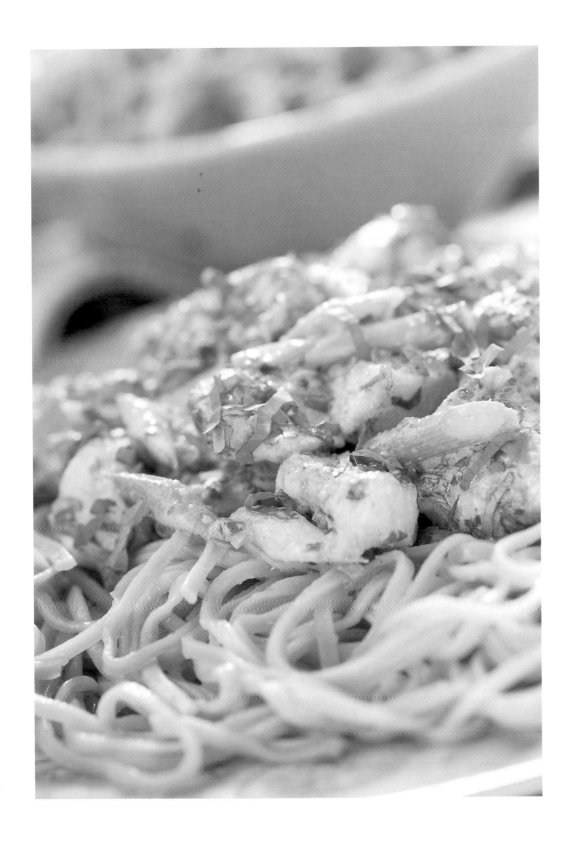

chicken with
lemon-grass & chilli

very easy	
serves 4	
10 minutes	
50 minutes	

ingredients

2 tbsp vegetable oil
4 garlic cloves, sliced thinly
1 onion, sliced thinly
2 lemon-grass stalks, outer part
 removed, chopped very finely
2 red chillies, deseeded and
 chopped finely

8 chicken thighs with bones and skin
3 tbsp fish sauce
1 tbsp light brown sugar
225 ml/8 fl oz chicken stock

Heat the oil in a large frying pan. Add the garlic and onion and cook gently for 5–10 minutes, or until soft.

Add the lemon-grass and chilli and cook for 2 minutes. Add the chicken and cook for 5 minutes, or until browned all over.

Add the fish sauce, sugar and stock. Bring to the boil, reduce the heat and simmer, covered, for 30 minutes, or until the chicken is cooked through and tender. Stir occasionally and add water, if necessary. Serve immediately.

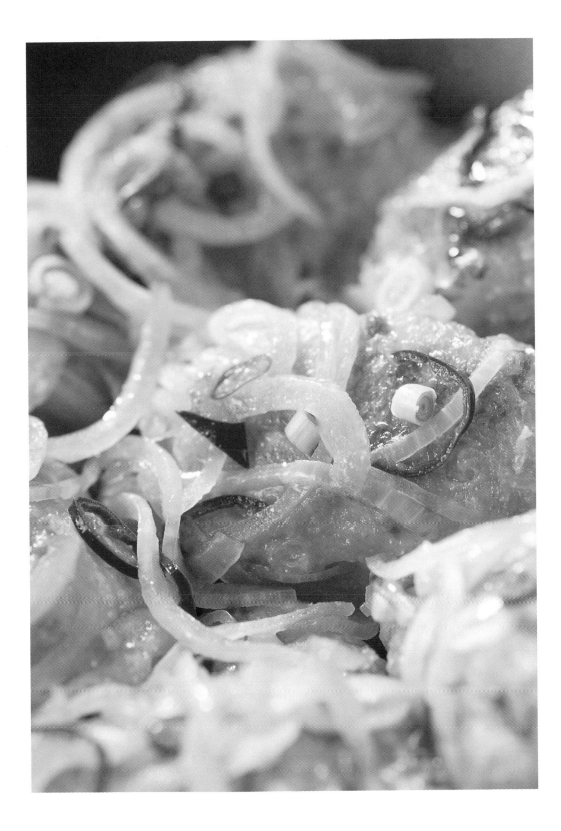

peanut crusted chicken
with dipping sauce

		ingredients	
🔪	easy	2 garlic cloves, crushed	DIPPING SAUCE
		2.5 cm/1 inch fresh root ginger, peeled and grated finely	1 fresh red chilli, deseeded and chopped finely
🍴	serves 6	1 lemon-grass stalk, outer leaves removed, chopped finely	2 garlic cloves, crushed
		2 tbsp chopped fresh coriander leaves	125 ml/4 fl oz white wine vinegar
🥣	20 minutes	175 g/6 oz salted peanuts	2 tbsp dark brown sugar
		115 g/4 oz plain flour	
🕐	35 minutes	2 eggs	
		4 tbsp milk	
		12 chicken drumsticks, skin removed	

Preheat the oven to 220°C/425°F/Gas Mark 7. Place the garlic, ginger, lemon-grass, coriander leaves, peanuts and 2 tablespoons of the flour in a food processor and blend until finely ground. Transfer to a shallow dish.

In a bowl, beat together the eggs and milk. Spread the remaining flour on a plate. Dip the drumsticks into the flour, then into the egg mixture and finally into the peanut mixture. Arrange them in an oiled roasting tin. Bake in the oven for 15 minutes, then turn them and cook for another 15 minutes. Pour off any excess oil and cook the drumsticks for 5 more minutes, or until very crisp.

To make the sauce, grind the chilli and garlic to a paste using a mortar and pestle. Put the vinegar and sugar in a pan. Heat gently until the sugar dissolves. Bring to the boil and simmer for 2 minutes. Stir in the chilli-garlic paste. Transfer to a bowl. Drain the drumsticks on kitchen paper and serve with the sauce.

roast duck salad

		ingredients	
very easy	2 duck breasts	DRESSING
	2 little gem lettuces, shredded	juice of 2 limes
serves 4	115 g/4 oz beansprouts	3 tbsp fish sauce
	1 yellow pepper, deseeded and cut	1 tbsp soft brown sugar
	into thin strips	2 tsp sweet chilli sauce
20 minutes	½ cucumber, deseeded and cut into	2.5 cm/1 inch fresh root ginger,
	matchsticks	grated finely
		3 tbsp chopped fresh mint
20–30 minutes	GARNISH	3 tbsp chopped fresh basil
	2 tsp shredded lime zest	
	2 tbsp shredded coconut, toasted	

Preheat the oven to 200°C/400°F/Gas Mark 6. Place the duck breasts on a rack set over a roasting tin and roast in the oven for 20–30 minutes, or until cooked as desired and the skin is crisp. Remove from the oven and set aside to cool.

In a large bowl, combine the lettuce, beansprouts, pepper and cucumber. Cut the cooled duck into strips and add to the salad. Mix well.

In a bowl, whisk together the lime juice, fish sauce, sugar, chilli sauce, ginger, mint and basil. Add the dressing to the salad and toss well.

Turn the salad out onto a serving platter and garnish with the lime zest and shredded coconut before serving.

vegetables, salads, noodles & rice

The vegetable dishes in this section, such as Stir-fried Green Vegetables, can be served as an accompaniment to the main course or you could serve one or two of the dishes with noodles or rice as a light lunch or supper. If you omit the fish sauce, they are suitable for vegetarians. Rice is the staple food of Thailand and plain cooked fragrant rice is served at every meal. Spicy Fried Rice is a good accompaniment to a plain main course or can be served as a dish in its own right. Noodles can be combined with a wide variety of different ingredients and are equally good served hot or cold.

stir-fried
green vegetables

		ingredients	
	extremely easy	2 tbsp vegetable oil	115 g/4 oz mangetouts, trimmed and halved
		3 garlic cloves, sliced thinly	
	serves 4	2.5 cm/1 inch fresh root ginger, sliced thinly	freshly ground black pepper
			1 tbsp fish sauce
		175 g/6 oz baby spinach leaves, washed and drained	1 tbsp oyster sauce
	15 minutes		1 tsp sugar
		175 g/6 oz broccoli, cut into small florets	4 spring onions, chopped diagonally
	10 minutes	115 g/4 oz green beans, trimmed and halved	

Heat the oil in a wok. Cook the garlic and ginger for 1 minute, then add the spinach, broccoli and beans and cook for 2 minutes.

Add the mangetouts and cook all the vegetables over a high heat, for 2 minutes.

Add the pepper, fish sauce, oyster sauce, sugar and spring onions and continue to cook for another 2 minutes.

Transfer to a heated serving plate and serve at once.

vegetable & coconut curry

easy	
serves 4	
20 minutes	
40–50 minutes	

ingredients

1 onion, chopped roughly
3 garlic cloves, sliced thinly
2.5 cm/1 inch fresh root ginger, sliced thinly
2 fresh green chillies, deseeded and chopped finely
1 tbsp vegetable oil
1 tsp ground turmeric
1 tsp ground coriander
1 tsp ground cumin

1 kg/2 lb 4 oz mixed vegetables (eg, cauliflower, courgettes, potatoes, carrots, green beans), cut into chunks
200 g/7 oz creamed coconut
600 ml/1 pint boiling water
salt and pepper
2 tbsp chopped fresh coriander, to garnish
cooked rice, to serve

Put the onion, garlic, ginger and chillies in a food processor and blend until almost smooth.

Heat the oil in a large heavy-based pan, add the onion mixture and cook gently for 5 minutes, stirring constantly.

Add the turmeric, coriander and cumin and cook for 3–4 minutes, stirring. Add the vegetables and stir to coat in the spice paste.

In a jug, mix together the creamed coconut and boiling water and stir until dissolved. Add the coconut milk to the vegetables, cover and simmer for 30–40 minutes, or until the vegetables are tender.

Season with salt and pepper, garnish with the chopped coriander and serve with rice.

thai salad
with peanut dressing

	ingredients	
easy	250 g/9 oz white cabbage, shredded	PEANUT SAUCE
	4 carrots, cut into matchsticks	2 tbsp smooth peanut butter
serves 4	4 celery sticks, cut into matchsticks	200 ml/7 fl oz coconut cream
	250 g/9 oz beansprouts	2 tsp red Thai curry paste
	½ cucumber, cut into matchsticks	1 tbsp fish sauce
15 minutes		1 tbsp soft light brown sugar
		GARNISH
10 minutes		fried onion
		sliced green chilli

In a steamer set above a pan of boiling water, steam the cabbage, carrots and celery for 3–4 minutes until just tender. Leave to cool.

Arrange the beansprouts on a large shallow serving dish. Arrange the cabbage, carrots, celery and cucumber on top.

To make the sauce, place the peanut butter, coconut cream, red Thai curry paste, fish sauce and sugar in a pan. Heat gently, stirring, adding a little hot water, if necessary, to make a coating sauce. Spoon a little of the sauce over the vegetables and then garnish with fried onions and sliced chilli. Serve the rest of the sauce separately.

green papaya salad

		ingredients	
very easy	225 g/8 oz mangetouts	GARNISH	
	2 unripe papayas	12 cherry tomatoes, halved	
serves 4–6	DRESSING	2 tbsp chopped peanuts	
	2 garlic cloves, crushed		
	2 fresh red chillies, deseeded and	½ head of Chinese leaves, to serve	
15 minutes	chopped finely		
	1 tsp sugar		
	2 tbsp soy sauce		
3 minutes	juice of 1 lime		

Place the mangetouts in a pan of boiling salted water. Bring back to the boil and cook for 2 minutes. Drain into a sieve, then refresh with cold water. Cut into thin matchsticks and place in a bowl.

Peel the papayas and remove the black seeds. Chop the papayas and place in the bowl with the mangetouts. Chill until ready to serve.

In a bowl, mix together the garlic, chillies, sugar, soy sauce and lime juice. Pour over the papaya salad and mix well.

Arrange the Chinese leaves in a large serving bowl. Put the salad on top and garnish with the halved tomatoes and chopped peanuts before serving.

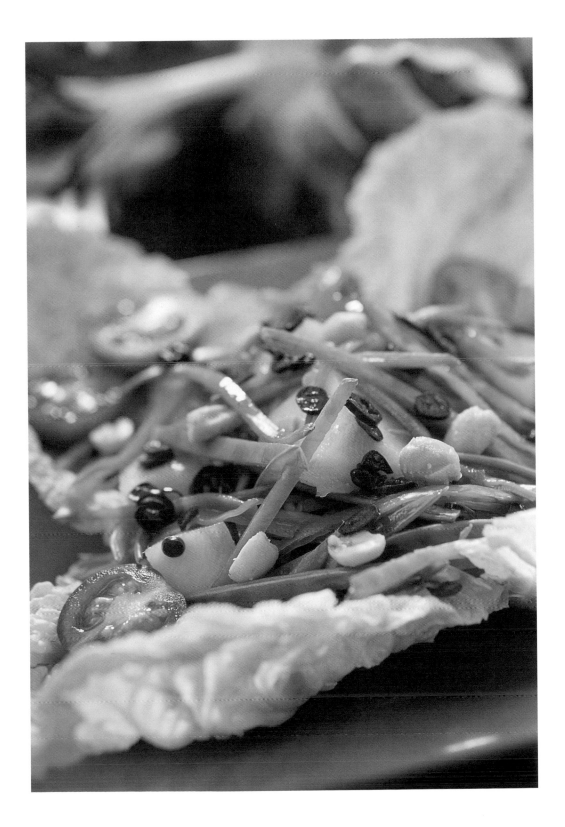

pineapple
& cucumber salad

		ingredients	
	very easy	1 cucumber	DRESSING
		1 small fresh pineapple	3 tbsp lemon juice
	serves 4	1 red onion, sliced thinly	2 tbsp soy sauce
		1 bunch watercress	1 tsp sugar
			1 tsp chilli sauce
	20 minutes		2 tbsp chopped fresh mint
	—		

Peel the cucumber and cut into quarters lengthways. Scoop out the seeds with a teaspoon and cut each quarter into 1 cm/½ inch pieces. Place in a bowl.

Peel the pineapple and cut into quarters, lengthways. Remove the core. Cut each quarter in half lengthways and cut into 1 cm/½ inch pieces and add to the cucumber. Add the onion and watercress and mix.

To make the dressing, place the lemon juice, soy sauce, sugar, chilli sauce and mint in a bowl and whisk together.

Pour the dressing over the salad and toss together. Transfer to a large serving platter and serve at once.

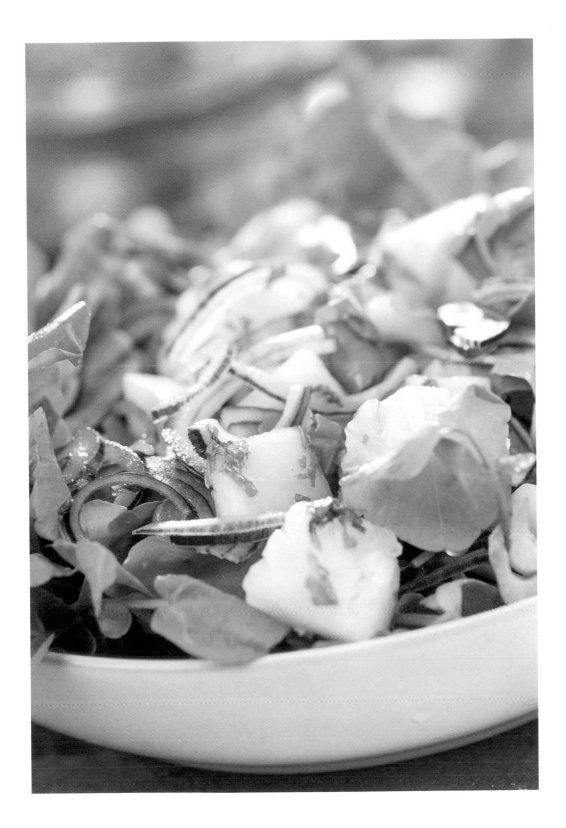

noodles with prawns
& green peppers

		ingredients	
very easy	250 g/9 oz rice noodles	2 tsp cornflour
	1 tbsp vegetable oil	2 tbsp oyster sauce
serves 4	2 garlic cloves, crushed	1 tbsp fish sauce
	1 fresh red chilli, deseeded and sliced thinly	1 tsp sugar
10 minutes	1 green pepper, deseeded and sliced thinly	250 ml/9 fl oz chicken stock
	6 spring onions, chopped roughly	250 g/9 oz small cooked prawns, shelled
10 minutes		

Prepare the noodles as directed on the packet, drain, refresh under cold water and drain again.

Heat the oil in a wok. Add the garlic, chilli, pepper and spring onions. Cook for 1 minute, then remove from the wok to a plate and set aside.

Blend the cornflour with a little water and add to the wok with the oyster sauce, fish sauce, sugar and stock. Stir over a medium heat until the mixture boils and thickens.

Return the pepper and spring onion mixture to the wok with the prawns and noodles. Cook, stirring, for 2 minutes, or until heated through. Transfer to a heated serving bowl and serve.

fried egg noodles

		ingredients	
extremely easy	250 g/9 oz fine egg noodles	GARNISH
	2 tbsp vegetable oil	2 tbsp finely chopped roasted peanuts
serves 4	2 garlic cloves, crushed	handful of coriander leaves
	1 tbsp fish sauce	lime slices
	3 tbsp lime juice	
10 minutes	1 tsp sugar	
	2 eggs, beaten lightly	
	115 g/4 oz cooked peeled shrimps	
10 minutes	115 g/4 oz beansprouts	
	6 spring onions, sliced finely	

Prepare the noodles as directed on the packet. Drain, rinse with cold water and drain again. Set aside.

Heat the oil in a wok. Add the garlic and cook, stirring, for 1 minute, or until lightly browned but not burnt. Stir in the fish sauce, lime juice and sugar and stir until the sugar has dissolved.

Quickly stir in the eggs and cook for a few seconds. Stir in the noodles to coat with the garlic and eggs. Add the shrimps, beansprouts and half the spring onions.

When everything is heated through, transfer the mixture to a warmed serving dish. Sprinkle the remaining spring onions on top and serve, garnished with peanuts, coriander leaves and lime slices.

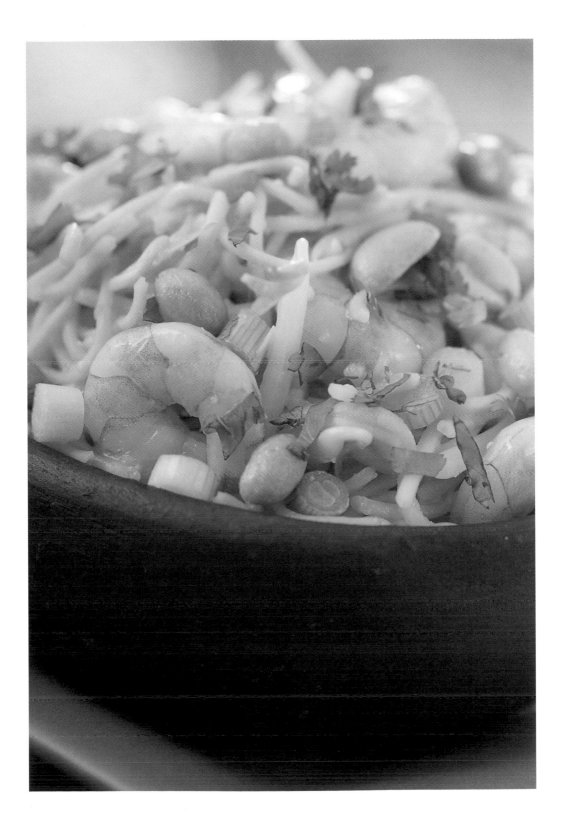

hot & sour
noodle salad

		ingredients	
	extremely easy	350 g/12 oz rice vermicelli	1 tsp sugar
		4 tbsp sesame oil	4 spring onions, sliced finely
	serves 4	3 tbsp soy sauce	1–2 tsp hot chilli sauce
		juice of 2 limes	2 tbsp chopped fresh coriander
	5 minutes		
	5 minutes		

Prepare the vermicelli as directed on the packet. Drain, place in a bowl and toss with half the sesame oil.

In a bowl, mix together the remaining oil, the soy sauce, lime juice, sugar, spring onions and chilli sauce. Stir into the noodles.

Stir in the coriander and serve.

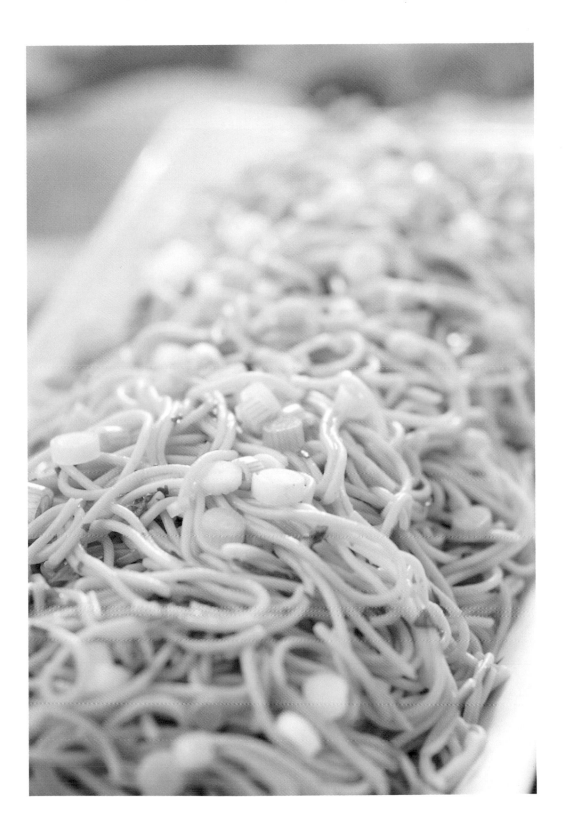

spicy fried rice

		ingredients	
easy	250 g/9 oz long grain rice	2 tbsp soy sauce
	10 g/¼ oz dried mushrooms	1 tsp sugar
serves 4–6	2 tbsp vegetable oil	2 tsp fish sauce
	2 eggs, beaten lightly	6 spring onions, chopped finely
	2 garlic cloves, chopped finely	450 g/1 lb cooked, peeled small
15 minutes + 20 minutes to soak mushrooms	1 fresh red chilli, deseeded and chopped finely	prawns
		400 g/14 oz canned baby sweetcorn, drained and cut in half
	1 cm/½ inch fresh root ginger, grated finely	3 tbsp chopped fresh coriander
25 minutes		

Place the rice in a sieve and rinse under cold water. Drain thoroughly. Add the rice to a large pan of boiling salted water, bring back to the boil and cook for about 10 minutes, or until tender. Drain, rinse under cold water and drain again.

Place the mushrooms in a bowl, cover with warm water and leave to stand for 20 minutes. Drain and cut into slices.

Heat half the oil in a wok. Add the eggs. Stir the uncooked egg to the outside edge of the wok. Cook until firm. Remove the omelette, roll up firmly and cut into strips.

Heat the remaining oil in the wok, add the garlic, chilli and ginger and cook for 1 minute. Add the soy sauce, sugar, fish sauce and spring onions, stirring to dissolve the sugar. Stir in the reserved rice, prawns and sweetcorn, tossing to mix. Cook for 3–4 minutes, or until the rice is heated through. Stir in the coriander, turn into a warm serving bowl and serve at once.

desserts

Desserts other than fresh fruit are not usually served at a Thai meal, but are more likely to appear at banquets and festive occasions. The dishes in this section are delicious at any time, whether served after dinner or as a snack at another time of day. These desserts are all light and most include fruit. Tropical Fruit in a Lemon Grass Syrup is fragrant and refreshing at the end of a meal. Coconut milk or cream are widely used in the savoury recipes in this book, but they also make creamy desserts such as the Coconut & Ginger Ice Cream and Coconut Cream Custard.

mango with sticky rice

		ingredients	
	very easy	225 g/8 oz glutinous rice, soaked for 30 minutes in cold water	2 tbsp caster sugar
	serves 4	250 ml/9 fl oz coconut milk	pinch of salt
	30 minutes + 30 minutes to soak rice		2 large ripe mangoes
	35 minutes		

Drain the rice and rinse thoroughly. Place in a pan with the coconut milk, sugar and salt. Bring to the boil and simmer, stirring occasionally, until the rice has absorbed all the coconut milk and is very soft.

Transfer the rice to a steamer set over a pan of simmering water. Cover and steam for 15 minutes. Leave to cool a little. Spread the rice out on a tray lined with foil, then roll the rice flat with a wet rolling pin. Cut into diamond shapes.

Peel the mangoes and cut the flesh into cubes. Arrange the rice diamonds and mango cubes on individual plates or in ramekins and serve.

coconut cream custard

		ingredients
extremely easy		4 large eggs
		60 g/2¼ oz caster sugar
serves 4		200 ml/7 fl oz coconut cream
		1 tbsp rosewater
10 minutes		fresh fruit, to serve
20–30 minutes		

Preheat the oven to 180°C/350°F/Gas Mark 4.

In a bowl, beat together the eggs, sugar, coconut cream and rosewater and stir until the sugar is dissolved.

Divide the custard into four ramekins. Place in a roasting tin and pour in boiling water to come half way up the sides of the ramekins. Bake in the oven for 20–30 minutes, or until set. Remove from the tin and leave to cool.

To turn out, run a sharp knife round the edge of each custard and turn out onto a serving dish. Serve with fresh fruit.

tropical fruit
in lemon-grass syrup

		ingredients	
easy			
serves 4	**LEMON-GRASS SYRUP**	1 honeydew melon	
	150 g/5½ oz caster sugar	1 small pineapple	
	150 ml/5 fl oz water	1 papaya	
	2 lemon-grass stalks, bruised	400 g/14 oz lychees, pitted	
15 minutes + 12 hours to chill	2 kaffir lime leaves	3 passion fruit	
	juice of 1 lime		
		DECORATION	
		1 tbsp lime zest	
15 minutes		small handful of fresh mint leaves	

To make the syrup, place the sugar, water, lemon-grass and lime leaves and lime juice in a pan. Heat gently until the sugar has dissolved. Bring to the boil and boil, uncovered, for 5 minutes. Set aside overnight.

Cut the melon in half, remove the seeds and scoop out the flesh with a melon baller. Place in a bowl. Peel the pineapple, cut into quarters lengthways and remove the core. Cut into cubes and add to the melon. Peel the papaya, remove the seeds and cut the flesh into cubes and add to the other fruit.

Add the lychees. Cut the passion fruit in half and scoop the pulp and seeds into the bowl of fruit. Stir to combine, then transfer to a serving bowl. Remove the lemon-grass and lime leaves from the syrup and pour over the fruit. Decorate with the lime zest and mint leaves and serve.

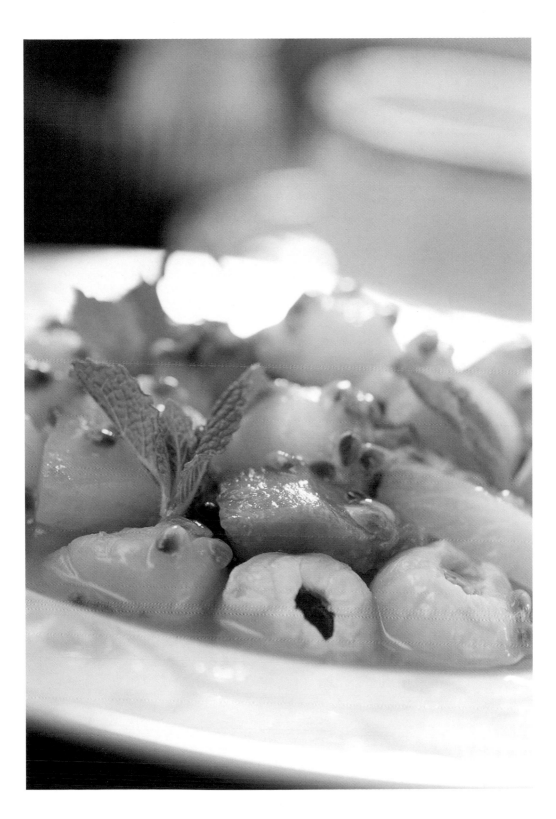

thai crêpes with papaya & passion fruit

		ingredients	
easy		2 eggs	FILLING
		125 ml/4 fl oz coconut milk	2 papaya
serves 4		175 ml/6 fl oz milk	3 passion fruit
		115 g/4 oz plain flour	juice of 1 lime
		1 tbsp caster sugar	2 tbsp icing sugar
15 minutes		15 g/½ oz butter, melted	
		oil, for frying	
		sifted icing sugar, for dusting	
20 minutes			

In a bowl, whisk together the eggs, coconut milk and milk. Sift the flour and salt into a large bowl. Stir in the sugar. Make a well in the middle of the flour and gradually beat in the egg mixture to form a smooth batter. Stir in the melted butter.

Heat a 20–22.5 cm/8–9 inch non-stick frying pan and brush with oil. Pour in enough batter to coat the base of the pan. Tip the pan as you pour it in, so the base is evenly coated. Cook until browned on the underside and set on top, then turn the crêpe over and cook the other side. Place on a plate, cover with foil and keep warm while making the remaining crêpes.

Peel the papaya, cut in half and scoop out the seeds, reserving a few. Cut into chunks and place in a bowl. Cut the passion fruit in half and scoop the seeds and pulp into the bowl. Stir in the lime juice and icing sugar. Put a little filling on one quarter of each crêpe. Fold in half and then into quarters. Dust with sifted icing sugar. Scatter the reserved papaya seeds over and serve at once.

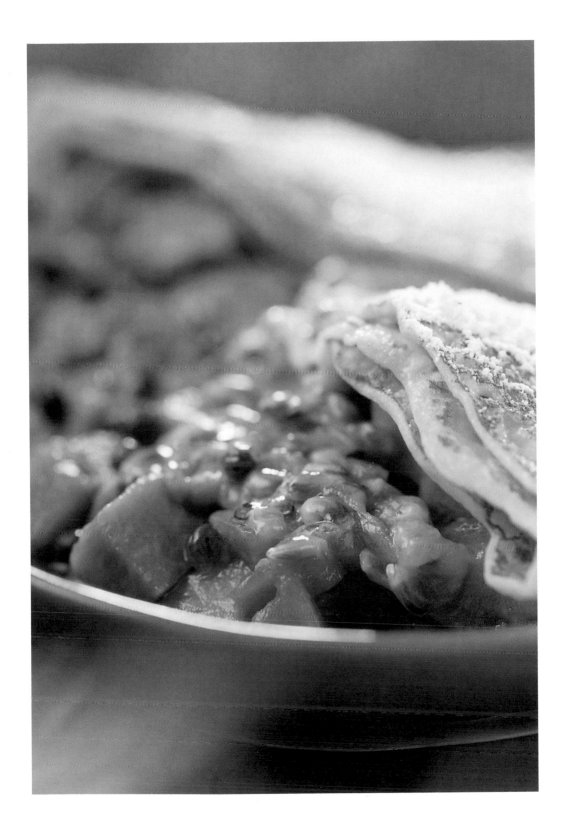

thai bananas

		ingredients
	extremely easy	350 ml/12 fl oz coconut milk
		2 tbsp granulated sugar
	serves 6	½ tsp salt
		6 slightly under-ripe bananas, peeled
		and cut into 5 cm/2 inch lengths
	10 minutes	
		1 tbsp toasted sesame seeds,
		to decorate
	10 minutes	

Place the coconut milk, sugar and salt in a pan and heat gently until the sugar is dissolved. Add the banana pieces and cook gently for 5 minutes, or until the bananas are soft but not mushy.

Divide the mixture between 6 small bowls. Scatter the sesame seeds over and serve.

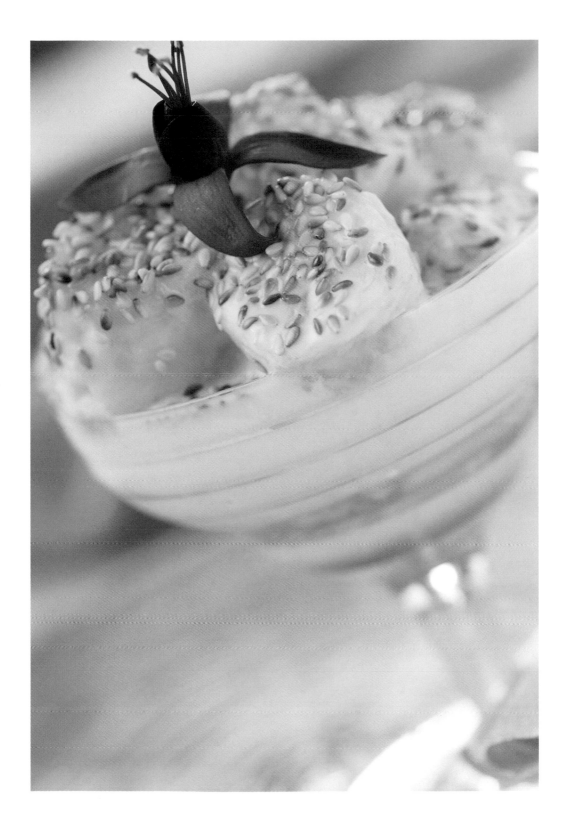

coconut & ginger
ice cream

		ingredients	
	very easy	400 ml/14 fl oz coconut milk	TO SERVE
		250 ml/9 fl oz whipping cream	lychees
	makes about 1 litre or 1½ pints	4 egg yolks	ginger syrup
		5 tbsp caster sugar	
		4 tbsp syrup from the stem ginger	
	20 minutes + 6–8 hours to freeze	6 pieces preserved stem ginger, drained and finely chopped	
		2 tbsp lime juice	
	10 minutes		

Place the coconut milk and cream in a medium pan. Heat gently until just beginning to simmer. Remove from the heat.

In a large bowl, beat together the egg yolks, sugar and ginger syrup until pale and creamy. Slowly pour in the hot milk mixture, while stirring. Return to the pan and heat gently, stirring constantly, until the mixture thickens and coats the back of a spoon. Remove from the heat and leave to cool. Stir in the ginger and lime juice.

Transfer the mixture to a freezerproof container. Cover and freeze for 2–3 hours, or until just frozen. Spoon into a bowl and mash with a fork or whisk to break down any ice crystals. Return the mixture to the container and freeze for 2 more hours. Mash once more, then freeze for 2–3 hours, or until firm. Remove from the freezer to the refrigerator 20–30 minutes before serving. Serve with lychees and a little ginger syrup drizzled over.

easy mango ice cream

		ingredients
	very easy	600 ml/1 pint ready-made traditional custard
	makes about 1 litre or 1½ pints	150 ml/5 fl oz whipping cream, whipped lightly flesh of 2 ripe mangoes, puréed
	10 minutes + 6–8 hours to freeze	icing sugar, to taste passion fruit pulp, to serve
	—	

In a large bowl, mix together the custard, cream and mango pulp.

Taste for sweetness and, if necessary, add icing sugar to taste, remembering that when frozen, the mixture will taste less sweet.

Transfer the mixture to a freezerproof container. Cover and freeze for 2–3 hours, or until just frozen. Spoon into a bowl and mash with a fork or whisk to break down any ice crystals. Return the mixture to the container and freeze for 2 more hours. Mash once more, then freeze for 2–3 hours, or until firm.

Transfer from the freezer to the refrigerator 20–30 minutes before serving. Serve with the passion fruit pulp.

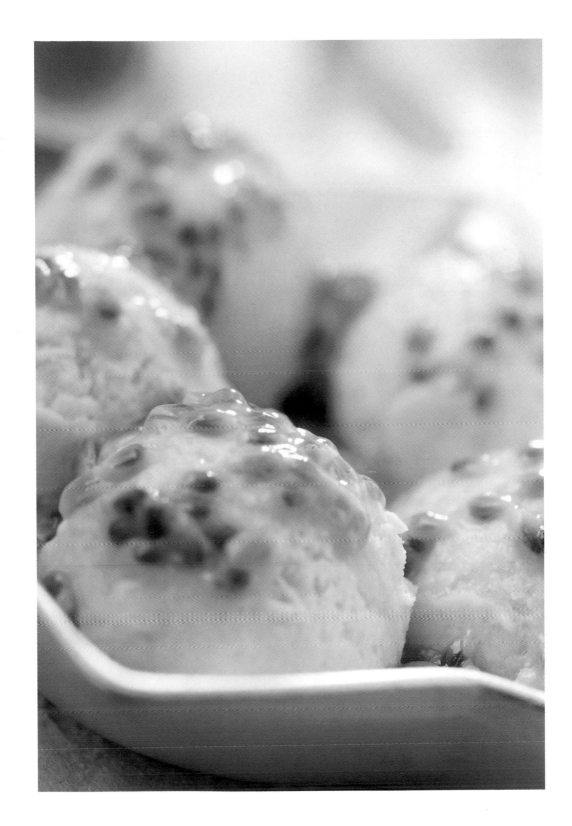

index